A HEROINE'S JOURNEY
Finding purpose while healing the wounds of Codependency and Narcissism

CHERYL M. FRANCIS

"Cheryl proves that great typography doesn't happen overnight. Truly an enjoyable read."
Sherry Hill

"Cheryl explains the impact of Narcissism and Codependency in such an enlightening way that even the layman can understands. It has certainly been a journey as I turned the pages of the book to see what lied ahead. I will recommend this book to all persons suffering from the effects of Narcissism and Codependency."
Wayne Joseph

"In the "Foreword" second verse Cherryl states - Our Blessings might be in a package we least expect and because we are so selective in our choices, we miss our blessings and spend the rest of our lives searching for or miss the blessings and opportunities. This quite caught my attention and is also a similar theory I have often used while helping my clients. I highly recommend this book to individuals who are recovering from Narcissistic Abuse."
Denzo Mos

"I am so very proud of this amazing work Cheryl Francis has produced. She has written a phenomenal book that is a godsend to anyone on their spiritual journey. This book helps you to get a clear understanding of how to heal from childhood trauma, overcoming narcissistic relationships all while finding your true life's purpose! I absolutely recommend this book to encourage and enlighten those on their path to spiritual awakening. All the things we have experienced are all puzzle pieces to our destiny!"
JaKayla Mason

www.highvibrationlevel.com

A HEROINE'S JOURNEY
www.highvibrationlevel.com
Copyright © 2021 Cheryl M Francis
ISBN:
All rights reserved. No portion of this book may be reproduced mechanically, electronically, or by any other means, including photocopying, without permission of the publisher or author except in the case of brief quotations embodied in critical articles and reviews. It is illegal to copy this book, post it to a website, or distribute it by any other means without permission from the publisher or author.
References to internet websites (URLs) were accurate at the time of writing. Authors and the publishers are not responsible for URLs that may have expired or changed since the manuscript was prepared.
Limits of Liability and Disclaimer of Warranty
The author and publisher shall not be liable for your misuse of the enclosed material. This book is strictly for informational and educational purposes only.
Warning – Disclaimer
The purpose of this book is to educate and entertain. The author and/or publisher do not guarantee that anyone following these techniques, suggestions, tips, ideas, or strategies will become successful. The author and/or publisher shall have neither liability nor responsibility to anyone with respect to any loss or damage caused, or alleged to be caused, directly or indirectly by the information contained in this book.
Medical Disclaimer
The medical or health information in this book is provided as an information resource only, and is not to be used or relied on for any diagnostic or treatment purposes. This information is not intended to be patient education, does not create any patient-physician relationship, and should not be used as a substitute for professional diagnosis and treatment.
Publisher
10-10-10 Publishing
Markham, ON
Canada
Printed in Canada and the United States of America

www.highvibrationlevel.com

This book is dedicated to my mother, sisters, daughter, son, grandkids, classmates, co-workers, colleagues, and mentors at Market America and Shop.com and all the persons who have affected my life in one way or another. To all the victims out there who are negatively affected by codependency and narcissism, "Lift your head up and have faith that God and the Universe got your back."

www.highvibrationlevel.com

Table of Contents

Foreword……………………………………………...7

Acknowledgment…………………….……………..10

Stage 1: Departure……………………………….…..13

Chapter1: The Parent-Child Relationship……...…14

Chaper 2: Narcissism & Codependency…………..25

Stage : Initiation……………………………………..38

Chapter 3: Cause & Effect Of Trauma……………..39

Chaper 4: Dark Night Of The Soul………………...49

Chapter 5: Self Love………………………………...59

Chapter 5: Being Woke……………………………..66

Chapter 7: Ying Yang Duality……………………...75

Stage 3: Return………………………………………83

Chaper 8: Let Go & Let God………………………..84

Chapter 9: Breakthrough…………………………...91

Chapter 10: Kundalini Awakening……………….100

About The Author………………………………….118

www.highvibrationlevel.com

Most of the writings in this book are my true experiences, but some of the writings have taken on a fictional and scientific basis for explanation and understanding of my theoretical understanding. Life is full of challenges, but we all have to keep the faith while we go through our respective experiences and know that a "Change is Gonna Come."

www.highvibrationlevel.com

The mythical story "The Hero's Journey" and its various stages resonated with me as I wrote this book. If one is to recap the Hero's Journey as it is vividly narrated by Scott Jeffrey. It is liken to Alice in Wonderland and Dorothy in the Wizard of Oz., who both started off on a journey to find out what lies on the other side of the road and encounters snares and thorns along the way. At the end of the journey, the victor comes away battered and broken but victorious. It is my hope for the readers of this book, as you, too, go through the mazes of life, that you find the rainbow at the end.

Foreword

Dear Reader ...

This book will focus on the journey of healing childhood trauma while finding purpose amid Codependency and Narcissism. Throughout the process, it is worth noting that people come into our lives for a season, a reason, or a lifetime and once the purpose is fulfilled, we continue on our path of self-actualization. We have to let these people go to be free to find their own purpose. Holding on for dear life only delays the growth processes needed. My mind is drawn to the story of the man who was drowning and cried out to God to save him. God, in His infinite wisdom, gives us what He thinks we need and not what we want. So God sent the man a plane, a boat, a submarine, a craft, and a rope, and he rejected all of them; and while he was drowning, he asked God why he allowed him to drown. God said to him, "My son, I sent you all these things to rescue you, and because it was not in the form you expected, you rejected them all."

The moral of the story is to be open and receptive to the lessons the Universe sends our way regardless of the package it may come in. Our blessings might be in a package that we least expect, and because we are so selective in our choices, we miss our blessings and spend the rest of our lives searching for or miss the blessings and opportunities. In the midst of trials and tribulations, the Universe may send us Soul Mates in the form of friends, family, work and church colleagues and acquaintances, or Life Partners -Twin Flame interactions.

The joy of life is finding a Soul Mate or Life Partner with the same core values as us, thereby achieving a seamless self-actualization process together as the perfect "Power Couple" that makes even Romeo and Juliet cry for joy. On the other hand, life could be made up of a series of hills and valleys as we maneuver the hurdles that life throws our way. Sometimes in life, we may meet our Soul Mate and Life Partner, but because both or one of them is not fully healed from the traumas of their past, they may have a "Soul Tie" together bonded by the traumas of their past.

If the trauma is so traumatic it sometimes linger with the person and affects their interaction with people; the trauma bonding that exists is fueled by Codependency and Narcissism, and the vicious and toxic dance is played out for the public to see. Well-intended persons see the relationship as toxic, but to the love-struck Soul Mates and Twin Flames, they see their traumatic interaction as love. Both parties enter into the relationship-wearing mask where their true authentic self is hidden. They both become Queen and King in a game of Chest where if the necessary healing does not occur, the final and ultimate destination is a fatal and deadly crash and burn of the relationship. To understand the impact of human interaction, it's best to look at it from a principle of nurture vs. nature – it's ancestral patterns (behaviors) clashing with universal retrograde (energy). What is going on in the world right now is the closing out of a 35-40 year cycle, with the year 2020 being a pivotal year because it set the tone for the next 40-year cycle. The change starts with someone in your immediate family and climaxes with an interaction with a soul mate, life partner, or Twin Flame in which lunar eclipse energetic forces pull the couple together in most cases beyond their control, all based on a Divine plan.

www.highvibrationlevel.com

Acknowledgment

I acknowledge the Management and Staff off the **10-10-10 Program** of The Raymond Aaron Group; when I was lost and wondering how I was going to publish my completed manuscript, the Universe sent Raymond and his team to me at the right time to teach me the "art of book writing". Throughout the three-day book boot camp, Raymond stretch me beyond my limits and for that, I am truly grateful. The lessons learned are priceless.

I acknowledge the management and staff of **EBookwriting Hub** for their phenomenal editorial and formatting skills. I am forever grateful to them for all their help. At times when it appeared like I was stranded and lost trying to self-publish the book they were a beacon of light in a dark and lonely place. I know at times I tried their last nerve but I commend their professionalism, patience and tenacity throughout the process and I could not ask for a better outcome.

I would like to acknowledge **Ms. Sherri Hill** for her immeasurable assistance with the first phase of editing of this book. You were my rock during many stressful periods and you kept at me to the end. Keep on being a shining example and mother to us wounded souls.

I would like to thank my friend of over thirty years, whom I call my "Big Brother" **Wayne Joseph**; you have been my rock and shoulder to cry on through some very challenging periods of my life. Not once have I reached out to you during my darkest moment did you not give me a listening ear. When I called you when I decided to migrate to Canada as an International Student and would have missed my Orientation Session, you didn't think twice; you volunteered to attend and collect the necessary material for me, and for that, I forever grateful. You are the brother my mother never had; you continue to epitomize what friendship truly is – continue to be the shining light that you are, "Big Brother."

A big thank you to another brother from another mother, **Martin Lewis**; you have been my role model throughout my ten-year journey here in Canada. When my other brother from another mother, **Reginald Lord,** called you to say "my little sis" is coming to Canada to study look after her for me," you didn't hesitate to take on the challenge of guiding me through the various hurdles of the Canadian system. I know there were times I tried your "last nerve," but you were always there to answer the call when I was stranded at the side of the road after a late-night class and desperately needed a ride home. You were also there as I went through my various personal life struggles and always believed in me even when I didn't even believe in myself. When I called to tell you I am thinking of writing a book about my journey, the first thing out of your mouth was, "Why not, you will be a great author." You are truly an angel in human form, and for that, I will always be grateful.

I would like to acknowledge Ms. Jakayla Mason – YouTuber, Mentor and Sponsor of Market America and Shop.com for helping me to connect to my purpose. Thanks to her I am now an Unfranchise Business Owner.

I would like to thank the Management and Staff of the various organizations and schools that have shaped my life in one way or the other and made me into the woman I am today. There were many life lessons learned along the way.

Finally, I would like to thank my mother, **Annette Francis,** and my kids **Chevon Francis** and **Brandon Phillip** for giving me some of life's greatest lessons regarding parenting and setting healthy boundaries. My patience has increased beyond measure, and you all taught me what it means to have unconditional love and acceptance for another. As we all continue on our soul journey, I ask God and the Universe to…

"Grant me the serenity to accept the things I can't change, the courage to change the things I can, and the wisdom to know the difference."
        Reinhold Niebuhr

Stage 1: Departure

Come and take a journey with me as we explore the maze of codependency and narcissism - while finding purpose in the midst of healing. Let us do like Alice and jump into the rabbit hole as we try to discover Wonderland together.

Chapter 1:
The Parent-child relationship

"A stable and nurturing childhood is essential for the healthy psycho-emotional and spiritual development of a human being. While we may understand what is supposed to happen to us physically, we must begin to better understand what happens to children mentally, emotionally, and spiritually as a result of the families into which they are born."
Iyanla Vanzant

CHILDHOOD WOUNDING

It is all good to talk about manifestation starting with intent. There are persons who have mastered the art of powerful thinking to the point of achieving goals in the physical realm. Yes, it can and does work for the people who grew up in a loving home environment where they were taught to express their feelings without being judged; or where their emotional and physical needs were not violated. Therefore, they grew up well rounded and balanced. On the contrary, those across the tracks away from home with the white picket fence live a child wherein their community is a daily collage of family coexisting - where the common theme of their existence is drugs, alcohol, sex, abandonment, and rejection, to name a few. The daily plight of the child across the tracks plays out this way - the patriarch of the home just received his weekly paycheck from his employer decides to pass by Miss Jane Doe shop and take a drink with the boys after working hard all day. The "boys" challenge him to a few shots of rum and a game of domino and in his drunken stupor, he humbly agrees.

In the father's haste to please the boys and satisfy his primal need for validation, he decides to put his entire 2-weeks' paycheck on the board with the intention of winning back more than he invested. Three hours later, he staggers home to his wife and kids in a drunken state disgusted with himself that he blew 2-weeks' paycheque gambling. So now he has to go face the wrath of his angry wife or partner who is anxiously home awaiting his return to collect the money from him to pay the rent/mortgage, pay outstanding bills while at the same time taking care of the basic needs of the family. But this can't be achieved because dad blew all the money gambling, and therefore the loud quarreling that ensues can be heard through the thin bedroom partitions by the now scared kids. The dead silence is deafening after the shouts from Mom are met with physical and emotional abuse from Dad.

In his fit of drunken rage, the father lashes out at the mom to ease his guilty conscience. Mom is then left curled up in a fetal position in the corner of the floor, rocking back and forth, trying to comfort herself from the emotional and physical abuse she just suffered at the hands and mouth of the person who years earlier promised to look after her and their future kids. He had so eloquently professed his love for her while standing on the edge of the green grassy track next to Mrs. Jane Doe shop. It's 10 years later, and those promises cease to exist. The young son - John, rushes towards the wounded Mother and tries his best to appease the distraught Mother with soothing words of comfort and encouragement while at the same time wiping her tears away and promising to "do right by her" when he gets older – and there starts the making of the Codependent Enabler.

One day while trying to appease the wounded Mother unbeknown to the other child, the father who normally falls asleep in his bed is now perched drunkenly on the edge of the bedroom door, through a maze of drunken stupor, demands that his daughter joins him in the family bedroom. In the daughter's naivety, she willing follows her father to the bedroom and, at the age of 10, becomes sexually violated by the person who was promised to protect her - and there starts the making of the NarcissistEmotional Manipulator. The mother looks on helplessly as the act occurs and, in her broken consciousness, tries to drown out the violation of her young child by using drugs and alcohol. To hide the shame of what happened, the mother further violates her daughter by asking her to make a vow to secrecy. The abuse of the child and the mother continues for another 5 years; the child later escapes the wrath of the mother by running away from home when she finds out the child is pregnant. The child later confides in her teacher at school that she is pregnant. The teacher tries to find out from the child the father of her pregnancy, but she does not spill the "tea." The pregnant teenager is placed into a "Children's Home" and, after the baby is born, is later given up for adoption so that she can continue to pursue her studies.

Another 5 years have passed. The girl child, whom we will call Jill, has completed her studies and while out shopping one day ran into Jack, whom she had not seen in 5 years. Jack grew up in the same community and almost the same dysfunctional home as her. Jack the Enabler and Jill the Narcissist did not get the necessary counseling and therapy that they need to get over their traumas. Over time they professed their undying love for each other because of the strong sexual attraction they had felt for each other. Unbeknown to Jack and Jill, the sexual pull they felt for each other was called "trauma bonding," and as they continue to express their love to each other the dysfunction of their childhood pulls them together and a "Soul tie" was formed.

Jack and Jill decide to get married and have kids, and the cycle of Codependency and Narcissism becomes an ancestral curse in the family. How can someone with so many traumas in their life overcome the hurt they endured as a child and operate from a High Vibrational Level to be able to manifest their intentions? I will say this would be hard to achieve without the necessary healing found through therapy, prayer, and deliverance. So it's 15 years later, and John and Jill have grown up – deep down, John secretly despises women, but he is somehow drawn to the emotionally manipulative women and is constantly angry because they always make demands on him physically and emotionally. Jill is physically attracted to men because that's what society dictates but deep down is emotionally longing for relationships with women because, deep down, she hates men, and so she is vindictive and manipulative and unfaithful in relationships, and she doesn't know why.

In the case of John and Jill, their attachment styles have a lot to do with the intimate partner they choose. Attachment is defined as the maternal and paternal connection between a mother/father and a child from the moment he/she is born. That's why in the western world, laying the naked baby onto the naked chest of the mother/father is so important to form that initial bond/attachment. The intention is to ensure the safety needs of the newborn; it is believed that this plays a pivotal role in the child's psychological and personality development throughout life. One's attachment style affects everything from partner selection to how well the relationship progresses and also how it ends. This is why it is important for everyone to understand their attachment pattern, which can help us understand our strengths and vulnerabilities in relationships and thereby avoid the inherent pitfalls.

ATTACHMENT STYLES

This bonding connection continues through the various stages of the human evolution cycle and is prominent between the mother and the child since, in most cases, she is the primary caregiver. Unhealthy attachments formed between the child and the caregiver spill over into adult life and impact the various connections this individual has with other persons. A well-known psychiatrist and psychoanalyst – John Bowlby, believes that there are four adult attachment styles that affect adults:-

    a) Anxious – also referred to as Preoccupied attachment

    b) Disorganized – also referred to as Fear-Avoidant attachment

    c) Avoidant – also referred to as Dismissive attachment

d) Secure

A child who grows up in a home with plenty of unconditional love from their caregivers, in most cases, displays a secure attachment style in adult life. The child grows up feeling love, acceptance, and value and therefore displays a high level of confidence when interacting with others and ultimately has equally healthy adult relationships and is not afraid to be alone; these individuals have high self-esteem and self-love and is not fearful of abandonment or rejection.

Babies and children who did not experience a deep bonding at birth and throughout life turn into adults who exhibit the anxious attachment style. They are fearful of abandonment and become emotionally dependent and insecure in their relationships. These kids grow up thinking they are not loved and have trust issues when it comes to the caregivers. When in the company of other kids, they are constantly scanning their environment to make sure that the caregiver does not leave them alone. For adults with anxious attachment, they see their partner as being "better than them," and the thought of living without their partner causes great anxiety in them. These types of people have a negative self-image and often seek approval, support, and responsiveness from their partners. Persons with this attachment style value relationships very highly and are often worried that their loved one is not as invested in the relationship as they are. They often bend over backward to make the relationship work, even if it's toxic or dysfunctional.

Children who exhibit avoidance attachment style have come to terms with the fact that they can't rely on their caregivers for emotional fulfillment and live their life feeling unloved and undervalued; they often perceive themselves as -"lone rangers," strong, independent, and self-sufficient. These kids, because they were never taught to express what they think and feel, grow up to be adults who do not understand their emotions and therefore do not express it and thereby avoid and/or reject intimate relationships. For those who do have relationships, their intimate partners often complain that these persons lack closeness. These people have high self-esteem and a positive view of themselves and often believe that they do not have to be in a relationship to be complete.

The disorganized attachment style is one that is a mixture of the anxious and avoidant styles. Children display this style as aggressive outbursts like breaking toys and fighting with other kids, and having a hard time relating with their caregivers. These kids grow up to be adults who tend to harbor anger and frustration. Deep down, these adults do not feel love and seem to reject relationships, although deep down, this is what they want the most, but avoid relationships for fear of getting hurt.

These various models of attachment influence how we as adults react to our needs and our quest to getting them met. For example, when a secure attachment style exists, one is confident and possesses the ability to easily interact with others; therefore, both parties' needs are met. On the other hand, if an anxious or avoidant attachment style exists and a person chooses a partner who fits this type of pattern, he or she will ultimately be choosing a partner who is not the best choice to make him or her fulfilled and happy.

When childhood trauma exists, it is important to do frequent clearing of the chakras. The body has seven chakras and has its purpose in creating balance in the body. The first chakra, "Root Chakra," is located at the base of the spine and represents safety, security, and stability in the body. When there is an imbalance in this chakra, it results in fears, anxiety, and negative energies. The second chakra is the "Sacral Chakra" and is located below the navel. It represents creativity and sexual energies; imbalance in this chakra is exhibited as sexual dysfunction, withheld intimacy, repressed creativity, and emotional isolation. The third chakra is the "Solar Plexus" and is located below the chest. It represents pleasure, willpower, self-esteem, and personal responsibility. Imbalance in this chakra shows up as lack of control, low self-esteem, misusing of power/authority, and manipulation. The fourth chakra is the "Heart Chakra" and is located in the center of the chest. It represents love, self-love and controls our relationships with others. Imbalance in this chakra is displayed as difficulty in relationships, depression, and lack of self-discipline. The fifth chakra is the Throat Chakra" and is located with the throat. It represents the ability to communicate and speak effectively. Imbalance leads to arrogance, shyness, withdrawal, and anxiety. The sixth chakra is the "Third Eye," also called the pineal gland located in the center of the forehead – between the eyebrows. It is represented by intuition, clairvoyance, foresight, and imagination. Imbalance in this chakra is exhibited as a lack of clarity and direction. The seventh chakra is called the "Crown Chakra" and is located at the crown of the head. It is represented as a state of high consciousness and divine connection. Imbalance in this chakra is displayed as disconnection with spirit, disregard for what is sacred, and close-mindedness.

Notes

Chapter 2:
Narcissism & Codependency

"I've always wanted people to know who they are from the inside. Then they can create the life they desire and deserve. I've always believed that my job was to facilitate the evolution of the human consciousness."
Iyanla Vanzant

MAKING OF THE NARCISSIST AND CODEPENDENT

The psychology of the human personality is one that has eluded human beings and scientists/therapists alike for centuries and still does today. Lately, I again felt the pull of trying to understand and analyze the human personality during the Covid-19 lockdown as the death of George Floyd resonated all around the world and how the "human race" rose up for a common cause to display their disgust with his brutal killing and after that with the death of Breanna Taylor and subsequent others. Why has man's heart grown so cold that he can kill another in plain sight, one may ask. Before I seek to understand this from a Psychoanalytical level, I will take a small journey back in time and see what early theorists on human personality had to say. My mind is drawn to the psychologist Sigmund Freud; years ago, when I started on my journey to University life, my mind was boggled with the idea of Psychiatry as a Career Path.

In 1989, I started part-time at St. George's University in Grenada, taking part-time courses in Normal and Abnormal Psychology, and was both fascinated and intrigued by the theories developed by Freud. It was in studying Psychology that I realized I had empathic qualities which would make me ill-equipped to adequately separate my personal feelings from my job of psychotherapy. So I made the switch from Psychology to Business Administration and lately to Supply Chain Management. Although I had put the matter of psychology as a career to rest years ago, it still had some impact and formed the basis for the analysis of the personalities of whom I closely interacted.

According to Freud, our personality develops from the interactions among what he proposed as the three fundamental structures of the human mind: the id, ego, and superego. Conflicts among these three structures and our efforts to find balance among what each of them "desires" determine how we behave and approach the world. What balance we strike in any given situation determines how we will resolve the conflict between two overarching behavioral tendencies: our biological aggressive and pleasure-seeking drives vs. our socialized internal control over those drives.

According to Freud, conflict occurs in the mind when the Ego could no longer create a balance between the pleasure-seeking behavior of the ID and the moral conscience of the Superego. The Id, Ego, and Superego all operate from a subconscious level where they are all ruled by free will.

When God breathed into man the breath of life, He all made us with free will to be able to choose right from wrong. Still, many of us choose the easy path and succumb to the will of the flesh and later find ourselves in compromising situations that we find hard to get out of at times.

I Believe that there is a strong correlation with Sigmund Freud Theory of the ID, Ego, and Superego when it comes to modern studies on Narcissism and Codependency. The only difference is that Freud set his premise on a Sexual Basis, but if we were to replace

Sex with alcoholism, drugs, greed, ethnicity, race, religion, culture, etc., the outcome would be the same. From my perception, the people who suffer from Narcissisism and Codependency are people who are disconnected from the Superego and are now ruled by the primal nature of the ID and a sense of entitlement showing up as an inflated ego. What caused this imbalance, one may ask? I believe that the advent of the internet by means of social media has caused people to see each other and their accomplishments from a close-up point of view. So gone are the days when people will climb the steps of accomplishment through Maslow's hierarchy of needs. People no longer want to go through the trials and tribulations involved to get to a sense of self-actualization. Instead, they stay in the dark and watch and watch and envy and bitterness develop in their hearts while they watch their counterparts enjoying the fruits of their labor; because they are not privy to the hard work their friends put in behind the scenes or how much times they are in their "pray closets" manifesting their intent. Instead, they let sin enter their heart through envy and jealousy. They plot and come up with devious measures to fulfill their lack of purpose, stealing the positive energy of their prosperous counterpart become the order of the day.

   Physically stealing from their friends will land them in problems with the law, so instead, they devise unseen devious ways to keep each other down hence the rise in witchcraft, codependency, and narcissism over the years. Man's heart has become hard, and as a result, they operate from a psychical/3d realm where their vibrational level is low. People have disconnected from their sense of self where they no long to hear the voice of God. They are no longer able to tap into their consciousness and make good decisions; instead, they operate from a fickle point of view where they are easily swayed by the habits and opinions of others. Competition and coveting of thy neighbors' goods have become the other of the day. Manifestation can't occur until the necessary healing, and spiritual awakening have occurred. A healed and transformed mind can have positive instead of negative outcomes. What you think becomes your prophecy or reality, is it a coincidence, therefore, that the Bible has so many verses on writing the vision and visualizing it into existence.

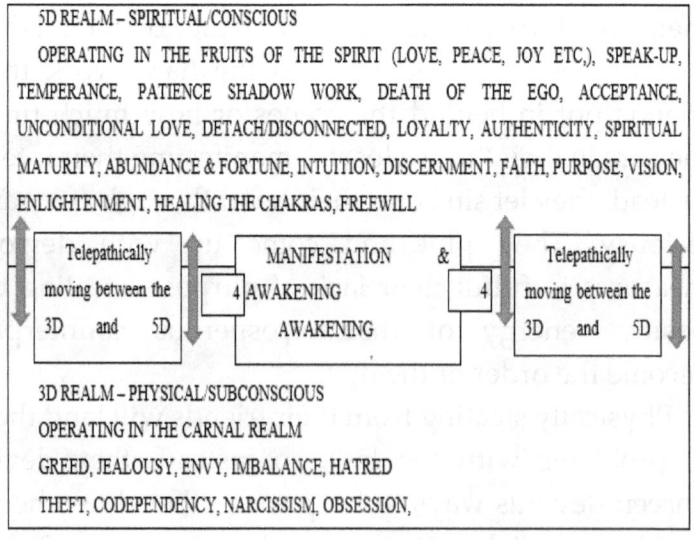

It is my opinion the Narcissist has the same traits as an Emotional Manipulator and a Sociopath. The only difference between the two is that one is Covert and might be considered a Shape Shifter; while the other is Overt and more deadly and sinister and goes against social norms and guidelines and will break the law to commit a crime, not thinking of the consequences for his or her action in the process. The sociopath is fueled with rage and becomes a law onto themselves and adjudicator. They believe strongly in a particular cause and belief and may go all out to prove themselves right.

Take, for instance, the people that don't believe that "Black People" are human beings and therefore should not be treated equally and should be hunted down and killed. So the recantation of the "Hunger Games" begins, and the aim is to eliminate all black people from the planet. Is it any wonder with the onset of the Covid-19 virus with people being locked up for so long that the Sociopath has had the time to develop more evil and sinister plots to get rid of black people from the planet. Is it any wonder that soon after the lockdown is raised that George Floyd is killed so sadistically. Is it a surprise that Breana Taylor and Aubrey Arman and the alike have been gunned down so callously? I, for sure, am not surprised. I am also not surprised that there has been an increase in divorce and domestic violence during the lockdown than before. Victims of physical and emotional abuse have been out of the homes more often and protected by social systems. Being home together has opened

Pandora's box and let out a plethora of demons that were lying within, so is it any wonder that the emotional and physical violence of children, women, and men alike has increased? Again, I am not surprised.

The Shapeshifters that were disguising themselves in the workplace, church, community groups, etc., and putting on a front to appease society are now in lockdown where they don't have to hide and put on the false mask anymore, and their true feelings and authentic self can now shine. With the mask off, the making of their twisted plots is crafted and brewed in their minds, and everything that they have been bottling up for so long spills out and over unto their family members and society at large during and after the lockdown. I strongly believe that there is a larger percentage of sociopaths and emotional manipulators out there that put down sinister plots every day than the media and lawmakers' report.

In my opinion, the emotional manipulators are the deadlier of the two because they leave no physical scars. They fly under the radar and go undetected for a long time until the victims find a way to become stronger and fight back, and the emotional manipulators become angered and enraged until they lose control and become physical to the point where their crimes are reported. They are so crafty that they will make sure no physical scars are visible to the police and loved ones. These abusers are also able to even convince the police that the victim is the crazy one, and what happened was not so bad as was reported. Again, because the majority of the scars are internal and not external, in most cases, the perpetrator gets away with a tap on the wrist and a warning not to repeat the crime. After the doors are closed, and the police have left the driveway, the wrath of the perpetrator is again released onto the victim in a deadlier form than before; that leaves the victim so emotionally scarred to the point where they are afraid to call 911 and report the crime again. So is it any wonder that the children in these homes who are on the receiving end of the manipulation grows up to become Narcissist themselves. The saying goes, "hurt people hurt people.

I believe that demonic spirits enter into the human body through open portals – if a child or person was sexually molested or suffered severe trauma, their spirit becomes wounded, and it's easy for the devil and his demons – the Jezebel Spirit and Ahab Spirit to take over their soul, and this person's behavior is displayed as Narcissism and Codependency (Emotional Manipulation).

No matter how much you may love the Codependent and Narcissist, you can't change them. Only the grace of God can renew and transform their mind and life. They first has to reach the point of rock bottom, and this mostly occurs when the enablers in their lives have had enough of their behavior and slowly start to walk away. After prolonged denial and hitting rock bottom, they choose to look inside and see the things in them that they need to change and let go and let God have His way in their life. They will begin the journey of transformation like the caterpillar who transformed into a butterfly. While the person is going through their breaking period, we, the enablers, will be tempted to help them and free them from the pain, but like the butterfly, they have to go through their transformation process.

If we say that we have no sin, we deceive ourselves, and the truth is not in us. The journey to balance, self-love, self-actualization, and operating from 5D starts with healing the Inner wounded child by cutting the cords that have us bound. It can start with mindful meditations; that way, you open up your heart chakra to let unforgiveness flow out and forgiveness flow in and thereby free yourself from whatever Soul Contract the other person had with you. In so doing you therefore, release them into the Universe for them to learn the lessons on their own that that have to deal with; thereby freeing yourself to receive the abundance the universe has in store for you because you took the time to do the healing required. For those who do not believe in meditation, the same can be achieved through daily reading of the bible and praying to God and forgiving the person who did you wrong or stating an affirmation continually like the serenity prayer or chanting a Psalm a day for example.

If the person you are dealing with is operating from a place of wounding and emotional immaturity one has to exercise patience and forgiveness to deal with them. For me as an Aquarians I don't have the ability to tolerate a person's repeated dysfunction; after repeatedly talking to them about the same thing I switch off and its something I am working on. Aquarians have a light switch in their brain that will cut people off without a blink of remorse. We show our love in an action-oriented type of way. We are not the feely verbal people. Our Humanitarian and Empathetic nature makes people take us for granted. We are all energetically connected, and that's how God made us. In the case of the soul mate, they may not be physically connected but connected energetically. If you fail to do the necessary work that the Universe sent people to teach, then since God gave each one of us free will, He will leave us alone for a while then put situations in our lives to make us reach rock bottom and allow us to deal with the Karma that our disobedience and irresponsibility have caused. The bible says touch, not the Lord's anointed, and do His prophets no wrong. So if someone intentionally does something to the child of God, God will make sure that karma is served, and it will be swift and painful on the part of the receiver. God sees and knows all things; what is in the dark will eventually come to light. God said in His word that He is a jealous God.

    The connection between you and your twin may feel so strong. It may feel like a past life connection – like King Solomon and Queen of Sheba. The devil is the master of manipulation, and he might disguise himself as your twin flame/soul mate to bring you down because he doesn't want you to achieve God's purpose in your life. The twin flame/soul mate may come across as a jealous fake friend. Peter was one of Jesus' disciples, and he denied knowing Jesus three times while Judas sold him for 30 pieces of silver. If you and Twin Flame had past lives together and your DM was deceptive, and karma was not served in the past life then in the reincarnated life the DM will try to do the same thing. Until the DF realizes the deception and takes the steps by using intuition and calling on God and Universe for protection and breaking the soul contract by creating karma for the DM and breaking the spiritual bond connection. Darkness and evil operate from a low frequency. If you operate from a low vibrational level, it's easy for darkness to enter through the body portals like sight, smell, hear, touch, sex, etc., and pollute the body. Operating from a high vibrational frequency frees you from the evil's grip. So it's time to tune out from the world by unplugging the TV, removing yourself from toxic people, etc. and go within and connect to self and the Universe/God and work on raising your vibrational frequency.

The Parent-Child relationship – especially the Mother-Daughter bond, is one of the strongest, if not the longest, relationship that has withstood the test of times. If it is healthy and dynamic it's a wonder to behold; however, once trauma sets in on the part of the mother – who has suffered abuse from the father by means of alcoholism, drugs, and sex, to name a few, this spills over onto the children who spend the rest of their lives reliving the trauma passed on from their parents if the necessary healing and forgiveness does not take place by all parties involved.

The trauma dealt to the ego of the Inner Child leads the child who later in life becomes an adult constantly seeking validation from the adults and children in their life and so begins the dance of the Empath and Narcissist by means of the Codependency dynamic of giver and the emotional manipulator. The presence of codependency in the dynamic causes a magnetic pull to each of the parties caught up in the eutrophic high that looks as loved; but even an innocent bystander could identify the dysfunctional nature of the pair. What lies at the root of this unhealthy pairing? one may ask, and the answer will be "TRAUMA". My mind is drawn to the analogy of the caterpillar, clay pot and the pearl which all have to go through painful transformation to become gems at the end of the transformation process.

Notes

Stage 2: Initiation

Jesus said….."My precious, precious child, I love you, and I would never leave you. During your times of trial and suffering when you see only one set of footprints in the sand, it was when I carried you" Author Unknown

Chapter 3:
Cause And Effect Of Trauma

"We really don't know how to love each other because we haven't really learned to love ourselves. In many instances, not all, it's not malicious. We've just been conditioned to such bad behavior."
Iyanla Vanzan

Let's take a look closer look at the cause and effect of trauma and the likely path to recovery.

CAUSE AND EFFECT OF THE TRAUMA CYCLE:
SPIRITUAL TIE + SOUL TIE+ JEZEBEL SPIRIT

ADDICTION AND CAUSES

Alcoholism	Sex	Incest	Tradition
Mental Abuse	DrugAbuse	Religion	Culture
PhysicalAbuse	Spending		

EFFECT Operating from Low Vibrational Energy Level: -

Trauma Bonding	Self-Love Deficit Disorder
Codependency	Rejection
NarcissisticPersonality Disorder/Toxic MasculinityNarcissist	Envy/Anger/Resentment/ Hatred
Psychopath/Sociopath	Witchcraft
Mental Disorder – Bipolar	Soul Tie
Suicide	Manipulation
Jezebel/Ahab Spirit	Cognitive Dissonance
Low Self-Esteem	Abandonment
Body-Soul Disconnect	

SOLUTION – BREAK EVERY CHAIN
DOING SHADOW WORK + DELIVERANCE + PRAY

Operating from A High Vibrational Level

Self Love	Being in Nature
Retraining the Brain Renewing the Mind	Prayer
Seeking Deliverance	Healing the Inner Child
Hitting Rock Bottom	Breaking through the pain - having a rebirth.
Clearing the Chakras	Listening to uplifting Music
Self-Affirmation	Counseling
Mindful Meditation	Developing healthy Boundaries
Healing from Narcissism and Codependency	Being Empathic

Let's go back for a bit to the love story of Jack and Gill. The chemistry and sexual pull between them were so strong; it was hard for them to resist each other. At times Jill saw some questionable characteristics in Jack, like wanting to know her every move and being so possessive and obsessive of her. The thing about it is that Jill is a free spirit because of her Zodiac sign of Aquarius, and she doesn't like to be tied down and controlled by anyone. Although she deeply loves Jack, his possessive nature was beginning to piss her off because she felt trapped. The reason the pull was so strong for Jack and Jill was that they were both trauma-bonded, and codependency brought them together.

Aquarians are Humanitarians by nature, and they are naturally empathic and full of life and energy. Although the Aquarian might have unhealthy or codependent tendencies, it will not be visible, and the Narcissists gravitate towards them because of their clean energy and become vampires and steal the energy from the Empath by making them their source of supply. But once the Empath catches on to the game of the Emotional Manipulator or Narcissist and does the necessary soul work, they transform into the Super Empath and cuts the Narcissist or Emotional Manipulator off at the knees by refusing to be a source of supply for them, forcing them to seek alternative sources of supply. The alternative sources of supply are not as rich as that of the empath. The Narcissist will try to come back bearing gifts and to pretend to be nice – but they are really shapeshifters transforming into what the Empath wants to gain supply need and again leave the Empath drained, and they are filled. So, it's important to stay on guard and on the lookout for the tricks of the Devil and switch to Super Empath mode when the needs arise.

The Empath mode is the best mode to operate in because it's the softer and humanitarian side of the

Super Empath. The Super Empath modus operandi is that of the crusher, destroyer, draw the sword, and cut

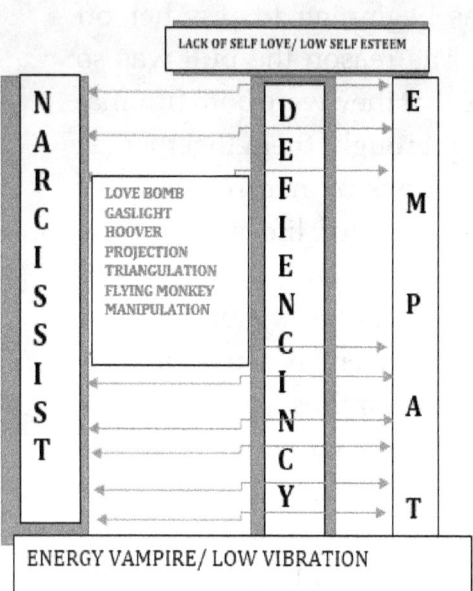
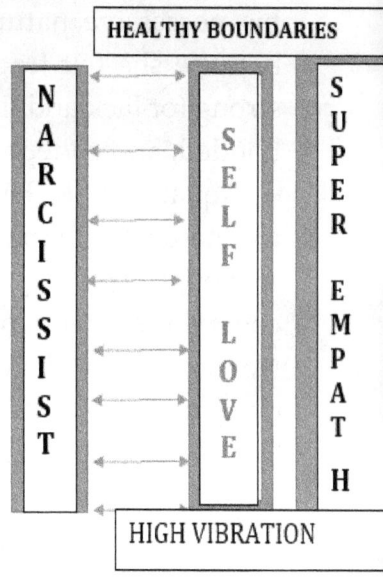

mode. It's the same as a mother hen protecting her chick and a mother protecting her child from danger, so in actual fact, the Super Empath is the Parent of the Empath. The Diagram below depicts the transformation from low self-esteem to self-love:-

The Narcissist leans on the codependent for emotional support and zaps the energy of the codependent, and the unhealthy dance between the two continues if healing on both sides is not done. The Codependent becomes the parent, and the narcissist becomes the child. This dysfunction will only stop when the codependent heals from self-love deficit disorder and walks away from the Narcissist. There are some who believe that the Narcissist cannot be healed by anyone. Only the healing balm of Gideon (God) can heal this person; not even therapy works for the narcissist.

A SENSE OF ENTITLEMENT

When parents give a child everything they want and do not teach them the differences between a need and a want, they inadvertently teach the child they are entitled to anything they want. So when they get old, and Mom and Dad are not there to give them anymore, and they don't have the means to get what they want, they come up with sneaky, manipulative ways to draw the wool over the eyes of people and take from their physical wealth or emotional energy.

Three stages of Narcissistic abuse – 1. love bomb 2. devalue 3. discard

Let's now look at the ways the Narcissists spins his/her web of deceit:-
a. Love Bombing
b. Gas-lighting
c. Triangulation
d. Manipulation
e. Jealousy
f. Fear
g. Flying Monkeys
h. Physical Abuse
i. Emotional Abuse
j. Lies

k. Deceit
l. Stealing
m. Gang-Stalking

The Narcissist is a wounded child deep down on the inside and is therefore attracted to what they consider bright and shiny objects (persons) and what is more of an attractive pull for a Narcissist than an Empath. An Empath embodies everything that is lacking in the Narcissist, and because he/she does not have it, in his/her quest to get those qualities, the Narcissist becomes an Emotional Manipulator and becomes a Shapeshifter and begins to pull the Empath in. The Narcissist, in some sense, is like a Serpent or a Fox who lines up its prey for the kill. Unbeknown to the Empath, he/she falls into the trap that is laid out before him/her and is caught in an endless maze with the Narcissist. The Empath is only freed when he/she taps into the inner self and decides to love his/herself more than he/she loves the Narcissist and evolves into a Super Empath to cut off the Narcissist at his or her knees by going NO CONTACT with the Narcissist through the Greenock method. My mind is drawn to the story of Tamar and Amnon in the bible, which could be linked to the mythical story of Beauty and the Beast. Tamar (Empath) was lusted/loved by Amnon (Narcissist) her half-brother. Amnon lust for Tamar caused him to lure her into his bedroom and then proceeded to rape her. Amnon then rejected Tamar by discarding her, which left her more wounded than the rape itself.

Get angry if you have but don't get violent and aggressive with anyone (punch a punching bag if you have to). Use Self-talk therapy, if you are afraid or can't confront the person that did you wrong - place a teddy bear upon a chair in front of you and pretend it's the person that violated you and tell the teddy bear how the experience made you feel. While clearing your energy field by taking deep breaths in through the nose and out through the mouth. Or write a letter to the person and mail it to them or burn it afterward. Do what you need to, to release the person from your life.

The Universe will send you help in unexpected forms and places. Because it may not look like what you expect, don't reject the help; take it; the Universe knows that you can't do this on your own. Don't be like the drowning man; take the help once you have discerned that it is genuine.

I remember going through karmic cycles with persons; in retrospect, I consider my "False Twin" and Soulmate. I had a deep love for both persons, and my love for them was tested on all levels imaginable. My character was assassinated; I was lied to and upon. There were acts of jealousy, hatred, gas-lighting, gang-stalking and projection; flying monkeys were used to carry out their diabolical plans. Everything related to Narcissistic Personality Disorder, I have gone through it with these individuals. I was so hurt it felt like one of my ribs was being removed from me because of the strong soul tie I had with them. Although I tried on my own and spoke to trusted friends about it, I still could not come up with a plausible solution as to why these individuals were behaving the way they did.

My only solace was to find comfort in the arms of God. I played gospel music constantly, looked at many YouTube videos, and read my bible constantly to the point where I felt the excruciating pain was beginning to lift, and like clockwork, I plunge into the deepest hole possible, "the dark night of the soul."

Notes

Chapter 4:
Dark Night Of The Soul

"The dark night of the soul comes just before revelation. When everything is lost, and all seems darkness, then comes the new life and all that is needed."
Joseph Campbell

UNBEARABLE PAIN

I went through the dark night of the soul in various phases of my life, and it is a painful and depressing process. It is one in which you don't know what to do with yourself, and it is in this time that you try to hold on to significant persons in your life. However, they withdraw further from you, but one thing I have learned through the "Dark Night of the Soul" is that you have to let go of the "EGO" in order for the "SOUL" to evolve. By detaching from the significant persons in your life, you get to connect to "SOURCE," some call source the Universe, God, or Zen. Whatever that may be for the person, the soul can only actualize when a detachment from the physical world occurs.

I found out after doing much research that the "Dark Night of the Soul" is an integral step in the awakening process. The stages of the dark night of the soul include:-

1. Great Despair
2. Questioning
3. Searching for Answers
4. Your path is shown
5. You find your Life Purpose
6. You meet your Soul Tribe
7. Spiritual Awakening

The symptoms of the dark night of the soul include:-
1. Excruciating Pain
2. Life seems meaningless
3. You feel like your life does not have purpose or direction

4. A feeling of powerlessness and hopefulness
5. You start to think of the existence and meaning of life
6. The feeling to impress others diminishes
7. You explore spirituality
8. You focus more on spirituality and focus less on religion
9. Childhood and past life experiences rise to the surface
10. You think about the principle of "Success"
11. Your Inner Child is discovered
12. You are less judgemental and more empathetic
13. You go through Sleep Paralysis
14. The mind is out of control, and you just want to quiet it
15. You notice a lot of coincidences
16. You notice angels/repeat numbers frequently
17. Your Life Purpose is discovered
18. You start practicing healthy habits
19. You start surrendering to the inner voice – God/Universe

What I have come to realize is that the Dark Night of the Soul is triggered by a traumatic life event – whether it's abuse, assault, illness, betrayal, mishap, or being the victim of cruelty. In my case, mine was triggered by the abuse from my Soulmate and False Twin. If we were to look at the world right now and the effects of one's mental health in respect of the adverse effect of Corona Virus a lot of people are constantly stressed and depressed because they have lost their jobs, while some are being emotionally and physically abused by spouses and caregivers and these events are enough to trigger the "Dark Night of the Soul."

The purpose of the Dark Night of the Soul is to take one on a Spiritual Journey where the Soul is united with God. In some cases, it begins with depression and ends with a spiritual awakening. If one is comfortable and happy all the time, there will be no awakening. It is in pain that one is forced to be humble and, through endurance, plod toward a higher calling.

The "Dark Night of the Soul" a poem by St. John of the Cross epitomizes the transformation of my soul as it went through the painful union with God. Prior to my transformation, my soul was slowly becoming black and bitter because of these individuals, and I thought of ways I could get even and give them a piece of mind and make them wake up and see what they were doing to me. I came up with a plan to talk to these persons. I told them exactly how I felt but to my surprise, they both responded the same way by gaslighting me and made me feel like something was wrong with me, and they were the victim. I came away from these experiences more wounded than I went in. It was in these two experience and more that followed afterward that I realized that the narcissistic traits were the same in all person suffering from NPD. The symptom is just hidden in different faces, shapes, sizes, cultures, and ethnicity, to name a few. I felt a range of emotions like rage, anger, resentment, bitterness, devaluation, and a sense of invalidation. I asked myself, "how these persons couldn't see what they were doing to me". I cried a lot in front of my friends and on my pillow at night as I try to reenact what these persons put me through.

One night, I remember I fell asleep in tears and had a dream where my body ascended and I was sitting on a throne. I went up into the heavens, and a bright light surrounded me, and I came face to face with God, and he said to me, "my daughter wipe your tears; what you are going through is part of the plan I have for you. The pain you are feeling will help you feel the pain of my earth angels constantly being victimized on the earth. You will be my vessel to enlighten the masses so that they can wake up as to what's going on in the world.

Dry your tears, heal your wounds and go back to earth and fulfill the purpose I have for you to do." I later felt my body being descended back to earth on the throne with a white light encircling me and my body leaving the throne and reuniting with my body lying on my bed. I woke up the next day remembering the dream and couldn't understand its significance. I paid it no mind. I went about my business, but the same experiences happened again a few times even while I was wide awake when I was sitting on a chair or in my bathroom in silence. It was in one of these encounters that I realize that God had a calling on my life, and it was solidified months later with the great loss and the sorry I felt with the death of George Floyd and the number of persons that were dying all over the world because of Covid-19.

DENIAL

Both the Narcissist and Codependent are in denial about the trauma that exists in their lives and therefore use each other as a band-aide to cover up the wounding of the inner child that has lain dormant beneath the surface for so many years. So when the two meet, the intense attraction formed through trauma bonding is often mistaken for love, and the sexual narcissistic gravitational pull to each other keeps them stuck in a soul-tie cycle for years without breaking free from each other. Even if they decided to leave each other, they somehow find a way to reconnect and continue the unhealthy dance again. Well-wishers in our lives see us falling through the rabbit hole and desperately tries to save us only to realize, like water, we slip through their fingers and down into the rabbit hole we go.

FORGIVENESS

Because of the pain, I felt at the hands of my Soul Mate and False Twin, I had to find a place in my heart to forgive them by doing the necessary healing required. I first had to start with acceptance. I accepted the fact that I could not change these individuals, and even if I wanted to, it wasn't my place to change them either. God made all of us with **FREE WILL,** and it's up to us as individuals to see that we have a problem and connect to source and do the necessary healing required. After reading countless books on Narcissism and Codependency, I slowly came to the realization that these persons and I had karmic lessons and soul contracts together. They were merely placed in my life by the Universe/God to act as a mirror or reflection of the things in my life I needed to change. I realized that I was not acting out of self-love because I was more focused on giving of myself to individuals tirelessly with the intention of getting back love from them. The more I gave to these individuals, the more they took and demanded with no level of gratitude in return to the point where I was emotionally and physically depleted.

The anger and resentment that developed in me because of **UNREQUITED LOVE** made me realize that there was something in me that was wounded and in need of healing hence the reason I was seeking external validation. I realized that what I was seeking was within me all along. All I had to do was tap in and draw from the well. The books I read and the YouTube videos on Narcissism and Codependency made me realize that I was Codependent on these individuals and similar individuals in my past, and their Narcissistic tendencies were draining me emotionally and physically.

Psychologists suggest disconnecting by going no contact with the Narcissist by using the Grey Rock Method. The Grey Rock/No Contact was of great help for me in my healing journey. Putting physical and emotional distance between my abusers and me helped me do the necessary inner work needed, such as cord-cutting meditations and spirituality work required to break the soul ties between these individuals and me. In order not to lose myself in the toxic relationship with Narcissistic persons,

DEATH OF THE EGO

My mind is drawn to the story of the man and the butterfly, which is likened to the death of the ego. "The man, in his eagerness to help the butterfly failed to realize the important lesson in the birthing process. In fact, the butterfly's struggle to free itself from its chrysalis is an integral part of strengthening its wings. The fluid from the butterfly's body is transferred to its wings, and once it is strong enough, it takes flight and spreads its wings and becomes a wonder to behold."

Butterfly Life Cycle Stages

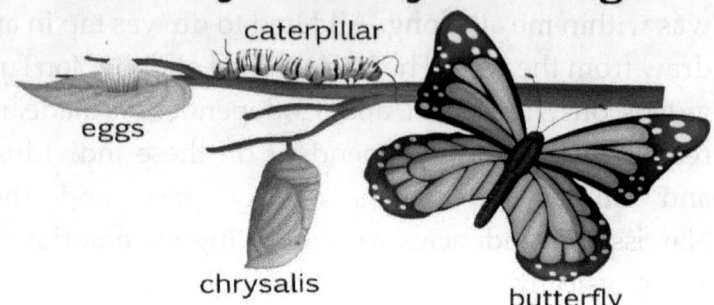

When we are going through pain, the people in our lives do not want us to hurt and therefore try to save us from the pain. Sometimes helping the wounded persons doesn't help but does the complete opposite. When something is easy, there is no lesson to be learned from the experience; it is during strain and resistance that we learn to overcome and succeed. Life throws at us a series of lessons or tests that, if we surpass them, allow us to progress and improve to the next level. It is only in the death of the ego that we can enjoy the joy and peace that connecting to source affords – **give a man fish he has fish for a day, teach him to fish, and he has fish for life.**

Notes

Chapter 5:
Self Love

"You have a right to say no. Most of us have very weak and flaccid 'no' muscles. We feel guilty for saying no. We get ostracized and challenged for saying no, so we forget it's our choice. Your 'no' muscle has to be built up to get to a place where you can say, 'I don't care if that's what you want. I don't want that. No.''

Iyanla Vanzant

SELF-LOVE AND ACCEPTANCE

Healing starts when the hurting person reaches rock bottom, realizes that the relationship or what they are doing is unhealthy, and decides to do the necessary cord-cutting and healing required. In so doing, this person's vibrational frequency rises and therefore no longer operates from the low vibrational level as before. It is during the healing that the scales fall from their eyes, and the things and persons that once had them bound no longer exist. In most cases, the hold is so strong even when healing occurs, the love that the healed person has for the Narcissist still lingers on, and somehow, the healed person is drawn again into the web of the Narcissist. That is why NO CONTACT/DETACHMENT is important throughout the healing process.

At the 3D level, because of the pain and trauma that persons would have gone through in their past, they are disconnected from their soul, and in so doing, they have left a dark vacuum where the devil came in and filled with the Jezebel and Ahab Spirit. So, this person who has un-forgiveness in the heart and is not consciously aware of what is going on with them displays Narcissistic and Codependent tendencies - like jealousy, back-biting, anger, resentment, manipulative and controlling tendencies, toxic energy, and the spirit of confusion to name a few. The person who is unaware of what is happening in the spiritual realm becomes so hooked to this person by their manipulative demon, and because in some cases, they did not do the necessary healing required, a soul tie is formed. This makes it hard to break free from the physical realm, and the person becomes entwined in a toxic karmic cycle with their karmic individual, which is being masked as love.

In some cases, the Universe will send us someone who will mirror our trauma and wounding, and to the innocent eye and observer; it looks like love, but the individuals involved are only connected by the trauma and the unhealed Inner Child within who is seeking to be loved and validated. Unless the necessary inner healing is done, together with therapy and spiritual deliverance, the magnetic dance between the Narcissist and the Codependent will continue to be exhibited in destructive and toxic ways.

THE JOURNEY TO HEALING

By going deep within and healing the inner child and connecting to "source:, you operate from a place of ZEN. That way, it eliminates the need to latch onto people for your happiness and passion. When you connect to your healed Soulmate or Twin, you both come together as two whole and filled cups and can unconditionally love each other without hidden agendas.

Those who took the mantle and ran with it and did the necessary healing that the mirroring is meant to teach them will remain in our lives and continue on the journey into the future with us. However, there might be times when no one remains with you because the healing process was too painful for them, and you have to continue on the journey alone. This time is when endurance and resilience are needed to motivate you on the journey and not stay stuck with persons that were sent to teach us life lessons because we love them more than we love ourselves. Therefore, we did not learn the lessons that they were meant to teach, and we are forced to repeat the lesson all over again. Staying focused on the work, abundance, and prize that lie ahead is what should motivate you to move on with the journey – dying to self is what the bible calls this process. Once you complete the cycle, you will wear your crown proudly, and the Heavenly Father places it on your head and says to you, "Well done my good and faithful servant, you have won the good fight of faith." As the saying goes, "you lose some to win some" same is true of the "Twin Flame Journey."

USE YOUR INTUITION

Go within and connect to the source, and God will give you a spirit of discernment to be able to identify persons that have bad intentions towards you and who try to place you in third party or karmic situations unbeknown to you. Because the narcissist can be so psychotic, my recommendation is that as you get the intuitive downloads, don't tell the Narcissist; keep it to yourself because he will unleash his whole arsenal against you and you will spend your time fighting spiritual warfare. Step back, take a deep breath and run like David did when the jealous King filled with bitterness and envy tried to kill him. This a spiritual battle that only God can fight. Read the book of Psalms and get solace in the words of David.

The Spirit of Jezebel is active in persons lately, and it's important to read the bible daily and pray so that you will be able to discern the spirit of people. Not all that glitters is gold; hidden behind the fake smile are the devil and his demons which lurks in the heart and soul of man/woman.

We must always remember that people come into our lives for a reason, season, and lifetime.

Steps to creating abundance:
1. Clear energy blocks
2. Listen to music only at a particularly high frequency 528 Hz+
3. Be one with nature
4. Do mindful meditation
5. Practice forgiveness
6. Let go of limiting beliefs
7. Exercise

8. Have gratitude
9. Offer up thanks and praise
10. Have grace for purpose
11. Put on the whole armor
12. Tune in to your intuition
13. Have a Spirit of Discernment
14. Tap into your energy – High Vibration
15. Practice Positive Intent
16. Manifest your intent
17. Have fun and enjoy Life

"Too many of us are not living our dreams because we are living in fear."

Les Brown

Notes

Chapter 6:
Being Woke

And he said to me, "Son of Man, can these bones live?"….. These bones are the whole house of Israel. They are indeed saying, "Our bones are dry, our hope is lost, and we ourselves are cut off!" Thus says the Lord God: Behold Oh my people, I open your graves and cause you to come up from your graves and bring you into the land of Israel, then you shall know that I am the Lord. I will put my spirit in you, you shall live, and I will place you in your own land. Then you shall know that I the Lord have spoken it and performed it," says the Lord.

Ezekiel 37:3, 11-14

SILENCE IS GOLDEN

In the great awaken process, it is important to remain silent and use temperance to be able to receive downloads from God and the Universe while at the same time observing people and things around you. It's like going into "the hermit mode" as you reflect on where you have been and look forward to what lies ahead. Some battles are just not worth fighting. It's better to walk away and live and fight another day. Not looking back in case you become a pillar of salt. The body goes through a lot during the awakening process. So, it's important to stay away from toxic people who will drain your energy and take you from your path and purpose. This is when the vision and purpose for your life have to be at the forefront of the mind while you manifest your purpose into existence.

Finding balance in the midst of the awakening is important and in the process the universe will put a mirage of people in your life who will trigger the things in you that are still in need of change. These people are meant to mirror us and are in our lives for a reason. A season and lifetime, and once their purpose has been fulfilled, they exit our lives. Unfortunately, those that leave have not done the necessary healing that they were meant to do through in the mirroring process; and the universe takes them away from us and the soul-ties are broken. It's a painful part as we look on longingly for them as they disappear from our lives. And it is in these dark times when we look left and right, and there is no friend insight, that we cry out to the father up above.

The death angel was roaming the earth in 2020 – it is no coincidence with what is going on in the world right now with Corona Virus and with the increased divorce and break-up rates globally right now. The masculine energy is under constant scrutiny currently, and those that do not straighten up and fly right this year will get some karmic whipping. The year 2021 – being the Age of Aquarius is where all dark energies get exposed, and those sleeping become awaken. Gone are the days where the Universe will continue to allow the masculine energy to abuse the feminine energy – Mother Earth is NOT playing with the masculine anymore.

Some believe that there was an end of the earth on December 21st, 2020, and the beginning and rebirth of a new world in 2021, and that those who are not healed/awaken and are not the chosen ones will get left behind by the Universe/God. The Universe sends people our way to walk the spiritual journey with us and mirrors to us the things in ourselves that are in need of change. In the case of the Twin Flame journey, it is believed that one person is resistant to the change and is caught up in things of the world instead of doing the healing. By choosing to release your Twin Flame and focusing on self-love, the energetic vibration that flows out of you somehow attracts your other half because it's "one soul" operating in two bodies. By detaching, you are indirectly saying to your Twin, "I have standards and wouldn't settle for less – I choose me." While you do the necessary healing and connecting with the source, you do things to raise your vibrations, such as - soaking in the bath salts and playing uplifting music.

Get yourself a vision board and write down where you see yourself in 1yr, 3yrs, and 5 years – manifest what you want into existence, and around these visions, write some positive affirmation quotes that will keep you motivated during the trying times of life while you continue on your journey of self-love. The bible says," Write the vision and make it clear." And remember to be gentle with yourself and others. When people come your way vibrating on a lower level, exercise wisdom by staying quiet. You now have the knowledge that makes you wiser – the bible says, "a people perish because of lack of knowledge." Remember, the person interacting with you is doing so from a lower vibrational level – 3D while you are operating from the 4D and 5D levels.

It's only through No Contact/Detachment and Separation can the true healing required begin. Staying together for the sake of love and fear only fuels the flames of toxicity and causes the Jezebel Spirit operating in the Narcissist to feed on the energy of the other person. At the end of the toxic cycle, one person comes away energized because their vampire spirit has been fed, while the other person comes away emotionally, spiritually, and physically drained. In order for a healthy relationship to exist, both persons must come into the union physically, emotionally, and spiritually whole – two halves don't make a whole, neither does one full cup fill an empty cup because one will always be filled and the other empty, or there will be two half cups which is not wholeness.

There will be some growing pains involved for both parties when the separation phase occurs, but in order for healing to occur, separation is necessary. Delaying the healing needed and coming back together will only continue the karmic cycle of the "narcissistic and codependent dance." Once the vampire spirit within the narcissist can no longer get supply from you because of "no contact boundaries," this may force them into the hands of another person, and they get their supply elsewhere instead of doing the inner healing required during the separation phase. Sometimes we have the tendency to look in from outside, and we see what appears to be the Narcissist living his or her best life with new supply, and we feel pain, become fearful of losing the person, and we take them back before the healing is done, and again, the drama continues.

There is a saying, "if you love a bird, you set it free, and if it was meant for you, it would come back." So let the toxic person go and focus on your healing. *"Que Sera Sera. Whatever will be will be. The future is not ours to see. Que sera sera".* Once you do the necessary healing, you are now vibrating at a higher level, and this leveled-up energy may cause intimidation and fear within the other person to the point where there might be a level of incompatibility. Once complete healing has occurred, and the karmic cycle lessons are learned, and once one or both parties no longer feel the need to constantly fight with each other; the un-

unhealed partner is then left to wonder where the partner from the past has gone, but it's because you are now operating from a higher vibrational level and they are still in the same old low vibrational level.

Sleeping with these individuals after they have been out there running around exposes you to STDs etc. Sage, your environment, drink plenty of water and play high vibrational music. Spend more time outside in nature, ground your energy by walking bare feet on the ground and also hug a tree whenever you can. Spend more time with positive family members and friends.

STARSEED/EARTH ANGEL

It was in my healing journey that I realized I was intuitive, and I had the gift of discernment, coupled with the fact that I was also empathic. Because of all I had gone through at the hands of many narcissists in my life, my empathic side had evolved into a Super Empath where I could smell a Narcissist from a mile away and cut them off at the knees. It was in researching what I was going through that I came across the fact that although I might be an Empath, I might also be a Starseed or Lightworker. I believe that me being an Aquarian, my purpose on this earth is to water the earth and to light the path of enlightenment for others to follow as this great shift that the world is going through right now.

AGE OF AQUARIUS

With the Age of the Aquarians, is it any wonder that there is an upsurge in the number of divorces and a rise in persons uniting with their Soul Mate or Twin Flames? There were some persons that were caught up in some karmic relationships and marriages that were depleting them of their energy and lowering the vibrational level of the planet. I believe that the Universe strategically utilized the events of the Coronavirus to create conflict in the lives of chosen ones forcing them to awaken to their purpose. Thereby remove themselves from the toxic environments they were operating in and to answer the call of the Universe to be beacon of lights to this dark world by being Light Workers through Humanitarian acts of knowledge and empowerment to the unawakened masses. In other to achieve the work set out for these Lightworkers, the Universe is calling forth the reunification of Twin Flames to work together and thereby raise the vibrational level of the earth by educating persons. Once persons become awaken all over the world, the vibrational level of the Universe increase, and the forces of darkness that is trying to cast a spell over the world and keep the masses subjugated will be crushed, and their plans become null and void. Mother Earth is crying out because of what mankind has done to her.

Notes

Chapter 7:
Ying Yang Duality

"Only those willing to walk through the dark night will be able to see the beauty of the moon and the brilliance of the stars."
Archbishop Socrates Villegas

DIVINE MASCULINE AND DIVINE FEMININE

With the Age of Aquarius being upon us, there appears to be a shift in the Paradigm and mankind is now on a Journey of the great "AWAKENING". Words such as high vibrational level and operating from a 4D or 5D frequency or high level/frequencies form the basis for human interaction has become the order of the day. What does all this talk about 3D and 5D mean? one may ask.

Let's take a closer look - The Devine Masculine or Devine Feminine; childish, promiscuous, philandering, and deceitful ways have delayed the spiritual connection with each other. The divine masculine lower self is in control of the higher self. When healing and balance occur, the reverse occurs. However, the reverse occurs with imbalance - obsession (passion, sex, non-committal, bread-crumbing, lies, deceit) soul-contracts (karma). When the Devine Masculine is behaving petty and childish because he is operating from his ego, you, as the Devine Feminine, is normally tempted to become carnal and operate from the ego too by cussing him off and giving him a piece or our mine. But unbeknownst to us, because God made him the head of the household, we are emasculating him when we do this – the same thing happened to David and his Wife Michael regarding the ark of the covenant. So what we as Devine Feminine have to do is remain quiet and exercise patience and temperance by letting go and letting God do the work needed in the life of the Devine Masculine.

We have to practice the same temperance our grandmothers did to their philandering husbands and that my dear divine feminine was how our foreparents were able to have a long-lasting marriage. Not that they didn't have problems, but the women knew how to disconnect from the masculine and his petty ways and tap into their higher source of power – God. By the time God finishes with our grandfathers, he sees the error of his ways and makes amends with our grandmothers. Patience is the key to longevity. The journey of the twin flame reunion is one that can be applied to everyday life, whether working in the office with our co-workers, church family, siblings, everyday persons on the street, etc. It's about coming apart to come together/reconnect in a healthier way. We have both a dark and light side – divine masculine and divine feminine and it's only in balancing both energies with us can we have balance in the outer world. It's about reuniting with our friends, family, and spouse in a healthy way by setting healthy boundaries and sticking to them. It is also about detaching from religion and finding Spirituality, and connecting to our higher self. The spiritual universe creates the physical universe. Change your negative intentions and claim what you want from the universe, and God will give you what you want.

SOULSHOCK

This occurs when one of the twins – "The Runner," runs away from the other, "The Chaser," because the Chaser brings up things in them that are fearful. The emotions for the Runner are so uncontrollably strong. It's not familiar to them, and like a bolt of lightning, they run because they are operating from an Ego perspective. In some cases, the DM is in karmic relationships and returns there because it's a place or normalcy for him. The Chaser is then left alone to figure out the dynamic of what happened in the relationship and recover from the rejection and heartbreak they feel from the connection. The Chaser eventually realizes through healing and soul searching that the other twin only came into their life to mirror the things in them that are in need of change and that no one can make you happy except you. Therefore during this process of acceptance, the Chaser learns to let go of the Runner and instead internalize and give to themselves the love they seek externally.

    The meeting of the twins activated all Chakras of the body, and all the trauma and fears in the body rise to the surface for both parties. The Chakras remain activated until healing occurs. When the twins come together, they will trigger each other both negatively and positively, but more negative than positive. Sometimes, the triggers may appear as Narcissism and Codependency. It is during this process that deep pain is identified to the point where it feels like a "Dark Night of the Soul." The Chaser, giving themselves the love they are seeking in the other twin, the runner increases their vibrational level to the point where they can attract a Soul Mate that is vibrating on the same vibrational level as them and therefore come together in a fulfilling relationship that the Chaser is seeking from their Twin the Runner. As is true of the Law of Attraction, as the Chaser no longer chases the Runner, the table turns, and the Runner now becomes the Chaser, but by the time the Runner comes to that level, the Chaser is already in a loving, committed relationship. It is therefore left to the Runner do the necessary inner healing that they have been trying to avoid for so long.

The wounding that occurs from a Soul mate or life Partner is hurtful, but I believe the greatest wounding that can occur is that from a Twin Flame, and this is another period when one goes through "The Dark Night of the Soul." The broken heart that one receives hits the heart chakra and resonates in all parts of the body, especially the soul. Some people spend a lifetime trying to get over this wounding to the point where the wounded person suffers from a mental disorder in some cases. I say at the times that God/Universe is humorous because He uses the experiences derived from the Soul Mate and Life Partner journey to test us through the Twin Journey, and if either party did not learn the lessons from before, these lessons are repeated in the Twin Flame Journey.

I can recall my experience with the Twin Journey when my eyes locked with my Twin Flame and felt a magnetic pull that I believed that the "Love at first sight" theory was real. Over time the sexual energy between my twin and me was so strong that it was hard times to resist. Around the time when I met my Twin, I was on a spiritual journey and was therefore practicing celibacy and was also enlightening myself about Narcissism and Codependency. Straight away, my body and intuition told me that my Twin was a Narcissist, but with the passage of time and getting to know my twin, he slowly broke down my defenses to the point where I began to doubt myself about him because he was so charming and empathetic at times. However unbeknown to me at the time that a Narcissist can be a Shape Shifter. I later realized that my Narcissistic Twin also embodied the qualities of an Empath and will shift between the two as the need arose. By this time, I had fallen madly in love with my Narcissistic Twin and couldn't believe he could do me any wrong; until I was stabbed in the back and being gossiped on by him. Those behaviors shook me to the core because I was not expecting this from him.

When I took my emotions out of the picture and took a step back to observe objectively. I realized that because my Twin was operating from the 3D level, he was driven by wealth and power, and when it appeared that I was surpassing him in these areas; jealousy and resentment rose up in him to the point where he felt the need to break me. So he began the quest of love-bombing and gas-lighting me to the point where I felt he honestly and truly loved me, and when I was vulnerable and let my guard down, he dealt the final blow, which almost crippled me. I had to go deep into the crevices of my soul to break the soul ties and cut the cords that were formed because of this interaction. I broke every contact and went into Super Nova mode as a Super Empath to ward of the continual hoovering of my Twin. It is my belief that my

Twin and I had some unfinished business from our past life that still followed us into this present life that is being played out today. I also believe that the Universe is protecting me from the onslaught of my Narcissistic Twin; while he undergoes the Karmic Justice from his past life experience. As he continues to resist the lessons that he is meant to learn, then Universe will assign me another/new Twin for me to continue this journey with. So in the meantime, as my Twin and I continue to be separated by time and distance I will continue to learn the lessons and do the necessary work that the Universe is continually sending my way until my accession.

Notes

Stage 3: Return

So we have come to the end of the yellow brick road - like Dorothy in the Wizard of Oz. Oooohhhh, what a journey it has been. We have endured the bumps and bruises along our adventure, and it's time to return home to put into practice what we have learned on our journey to transformation.

Chapter 8:
Let Go And Let God

"In my deepest, darkest moments, what really got me through was a prayer. Sometimes my prayer was 'Help me.' Sometimes a prayer was 'Thank you.' What I've discovered is that intimate connection and communication with my creator will always get me through because I know my support, my help, is just a prayer away."

Iyanla Vanzant

LETTING GO

The fact that the chaser is no longer triggered by the other twin by operating from a 3D level but has chosen to raise their vibrational frequency through healing and self-love, they now operate from a 5D level. In the 3D level, one is operating from fear, trauma, ego, confusion, and turmoil, but the twin that chooses to raise their vibration now operates from a Soul and Heart level, and the healed twin now has "Unconditional Love" for the "Runner Twin." Unconditional Love only takes place at the 5D or higher level, which means that negative energies no longer exude from the healed twin and the other twin feels the love. But Union can't take place with the twin because one is operating from the 5D and the other from the 3D. Because the healed twin is operating from a place of self-love, they are no longer willing to sacrifice themselves for their twin, who failed to change, and therefore, the twins remain in separation and operate from a friendship level. The healed twin then goes on to find their purpose and achieve self-actualization and ascension by being the best version of themselves they can be.

So you have done the inner work and cleared all your energy blocks, and you are on top of the world, going hippity hop down the street, reciting the words to "No Scrubs," and you run slam-bam into the arms of your Twin Flame whom the Universe has sent yet again to teach you another of life's lesson. If you are healed and level up, your Twin can no longer trigger you. What do you do when the words to "No Scrub" don't measure up to what you are feeling in your heart for your soulmate, our twin? It means that the process you have gone through with the Dark Night of the Soul is not complete, and you still have some more work to do. It also means that the death of the Ego has not fully occurred; and because of the residue you feel for your Twin. If you operate from a sexual level, and because of the energetic vibrations that exude, and you feel for your twin because you are not completely healed and the Runner-Chaser cycle continues yet again. It's in eliminating fear and worry operating from "death of the ego/death of the flesh" can true transformation occur.

UNCONDITIONAL LOVE

One thing I have realized from this Twin Flame Journey is that your Twin Flame is a reflection of yourself. Soul searching intends not looking for validation from your partner, friend, sibling, or family. It is about finding the validation that you need from within because it has been lying there all along waiting to be tapped in and explored, and it is with the tapping into your inner being that you connect to source and therefore find your balance and purpose that you need to pursue your goals and achievement in life. Disconnect from the world/matrix and connect to the source by taking the "red pill". Inner peace is found by looking within that way, no matter what may come to take you off course. You are so plugged into your higher self and vibrating at such a high vibrational level. No one with their 3D or 4D vibrational level can upset your balance or change your frequency.

Your 5D vibrational frequency is too high for them to reach and interact with you. Spread Universal love, the love you have to give to your emotionally unavailable partner. Transfer that same energy of love in a Humanitarian way by volunteering in organizations that deal with children, animal, or shelter and church, etc. Transfer the eros love to agape love.

Your alignment to God and Purpose affects your perception, relinquish control, and let God have his way in the life of your partner, friend, or family. There is more to the equation of receiving than just acting alone. You have to combine heart plus positive intention to achieve the abundant outcome you expect. Time is an illusion. You can work hard and still not achieve material wealth. It means one's view of wealth is limited. The bible says you have not because you want/ask not. You can work all day and have a defeated mindset. You will end up with more by changing your mindset. Once your intent changes, and you ask the Universe for the abundance you want, and the Universe hears you, and you see it manifested ultimately. Shift your mindset, and your outcome changes. Soul searching will bring inner peace to your life – reconnecting with source/God/Universe going within and find inner peace.

ELIMINATE FEAR AND WORRY

Our inner self will tell us the areas in our life we need to work on, and once you connect to the source, the Universe will send people in your life that will mirror the areas in you that need to change. The interactions will come across as discomfort and discord, and you will try to avoid these people to regain inner peace. If you do not take time to heal the parts of you that the person is mirroring to you, the Universe will keep on sending soul mate, life partners, twins flame to continue to mirror those parts to you, and the lesson will keep being thrown your way until you take the time to do the necessary healing and pass the test the person was sent to serve. Once the healing and test are done, the triggers will cease to exist, and other persons coming in will be trying in difficulty to trigger you because the wound has been healed and the lessons learned. Then it's time for the universe to send you another test and another lesson.

"Anger is an acid that can do more harm to the vessel in which it is stored than to anything on which it is poured."

Mark Twain

TWIN FLAME RE-UNITE

Once you realize that you are going through a test, you will take the necessary steps to identify the lesson you were meant to learn, pass the test in a quicker time frame and receive the abundance of the universe and blessings God has in store for you. My mind is drawn to Job in the bible, who had many tests, but because he remained focus and resilient throughout the process of his tests, he was given more abundance than he had before. Remember that there is always light at the end of the tunnel or rainbow after the rain.

There is a reason, season, and purpose for people sent or entering your life. In the case of the twin flame, the lessons are even harder because you both mirror each other and carry each other's burden. If one does the healing required and change; the universe may give the other party who need to change some time to do so, and if they take too long, the universe may assign a new twin flame or soul mate to the healed partner. In order to speed up the reunification of the Twin, it is especial to detach and connect to the source. Once this occurs miraculously, the other Twin shows up and wants to unite, but the more you hold on, the more the other twin runs, and the "Runner/Chaser dynamics continue. The Universe brings together twin flames to raise the vibrational level of the world.

There were times when I felt a tugging of my heart, and I was left trying to figure out if it was love or Codependency; during those times, I go straight to Youtube and listen to videos by Pastor Toure Roberts, and they have been a source of blessing to me:-

- 5 keys To Identifying Your Soulmate
- Love, Purpose, and Relationships

"The strength of a woman is to be able to feel things that no one else can. The strength of a woman is having faith in God."

Source: Saintpaulamanac.org

Notes

Chapter 9: Breakthrough

"We were all born with a certain degree of power. The key to success is discovering this innate power and using it daily to deal with whatever challenges come our way."
Les Brown

For a long time, I have felt the calling of God on my life, but like the prodigal son, this prodigal daughter ran. I ran because I wanted to party and fete in peace because I felt I was not able to be free to enjoy life when I was young. I, therefore, made a vow with myself from a young age that once I am grown and independent that I will live life on my terms, and in retrospect, I sure did. Looking back at my life, I had had an exciting and fulfilled one, although the area in my life I seemed to struggle with the most with was my love life. Nonetheless, I felt that there were more "holier than though" people in the church and in the world that God could use to achieve His purpose on the earth. I joined the ranks of people like Paul, Jonah, and Moses, to name a few from the bible that ran from their calling. I ran and ran and ran while exercising my "**FREE WILL**," like my predecessors, God forced me to put a stop to my philandering ways by slowing me down and caused me to focus within and do the necessary soul searching, shadow work, and healing that I refused to do because I had become distracted with worldly trappings and pleasure.

Like Jonah trapped in a belly of a whale, I too felt trapped in my home during the Covid-19 lockdown where I decided to look within and started healing my heart and the Inner Child within that was crying out for so long because of the trauma I had suffered throughout life. During the lockdown, I surrendered to the will of God for my life; I spent time with him, as I had never done before. I became vulnerable with him, and like Saul on the road to Damascus, I too was transformed from Cheryl into the "Chosen One."

Looking back at my past, I was betrayed by many persons I thought loved me. My heart was broken so many times, and like a wounded child, I became bitter, resentful, and closed in. I had a smile on my face but emotionally detached, and the walls I had put up, not even a "marching army," could have cracked my heart or break down the walls I had put up over the years. It took God chipping away at the ice chamber and using a blowtorch to get to the hidden heart chakra lying beneath the ice camber.

The spirit of my dead ancestors forcefully rose up in me after the death of George Floyd; his death really resonated with me to the point that I started questioning my existence on the earth and that of my fellow black people. Like a soul thirsty for the presence of the Holy Spirit, I began doing research and subtlety challenging what the media was saying about the reason for the senseless deaths of black people all over the world. I became like what my friends and family members will call a "Conspiracy Theorist." To me, as an observer of the death of George Floyd, 1+1 was not adding up to 2 but 3 instead.

I began to research my ancestral path, and the more I research, the more I found out, the more and more the pieces of my puzzle began to fit together. My purpose and existence on this earth began to fit together, and in so doing the more, I heard the whispering of my ancestors. I walked the wooded beaten path behind my apartment building after the lockdown, and the more I spent in nature; the more clearly I heard the voice of God and felt the spirit of my ancestors rising up within me. To the point I am sure I heard God's small saying to me on one of those walks "I have allowed you to party and enjoy life enough; now, it's time to do the work I have put you on that earth to do'" Of course in my rebellious way to which I respond "God what work is that? And why me?" and of to which He responded "You will know in due time, and why not you? Weren't you made in My image and likeness like all the other human beings that walk the earth," and to which I surrendered and said like Jesus, "Lord let Your will be done in my life."

Like Jesus when the sorrows of life weighed in on me many times, I said to Him, "God, if it is your will, please take this cup of sorrow away from me" To which He responded, "the trials of life are to shape you into the masterpiece that I need you to be to be able to do the work I have in store for you." Like a spoilt child I rebelled and rebelled and wanted to give up and the more I tried to give up, He sent lessons after lessons for me to learn and pass the necessary test needed to move on to the next level He had in store for me. Again, I could hear His small voice saying to me, "Cheryl, how many time do I need to give you the same test, and how many times do you need to retake the test for you to pass and move on to the next level, you resisting and failing is slowing down the work I have for you to do, stop fighting and resisting, just learn the lesson, take and passed the test and move on to the next level." And so, I have decided to surrender to the struggles and let His will be done in my life. And that "Road Less Travelled" had some thorns and brittles and bumps and rocks and mountains and serpents and wolves in sheep clothing, but with God's held, I continue to navigate the path and pass the lessons He brought in my path daily.

CONNECTING TO SOURCE

The first step to healing is admitting to yourself that you have a problem and in need of healing. For me, it was so easy to point fingers at the Narcissists in my life and identify what they were doing to me, but not once did I look at my contribution in the sager. Like Neo in the Matix, I made the decision to stop taking the *"blue pill"* and decided to take the *"red pill"* and start the journey to transformation. My enabling beliefs masked as codependency was the embers that were keeping me trauma bonded with the Narcissist. I finally came to the realization that I had a problem and needed help. My Codependency came from the Inner Child in me that was still seeking validation from my biological father, who from my memory was too constantly intoxicated by alcohol that he couldn't see his little daughter needed his love and encouragement as she went through the various stages of her life. My mother, who became the Matriciah of the family, was so overburdened trying to pick up the slack where my father left off had become too broken to realize that I was secretly crying out for love and attention. Although I had my family with me, a roof over my head, food on the table, and clothing on my back, I still felt like a lost and abandoned child without parents. Hence the void I felt deep inside followed me into adulthood to the point where the pain was reflected on my face for the world to see especially Narcissists.

The emotional pain suffered at the hands of my Karmic Masculine was so severe it took a lot out of me to recover. I was gaslight, gang-stocked, breadcrumbed, triangulated, to name a few; it took the grace of God to get me through the trauma. It was through the dark night of the soul I learned to lean on God and allow him to do the necessary work required for my wounded soul. I utilized my Amazon Prime Membership to purchase a number of paperback and audiobooks that have also assisted in my healing process.

YouTube also became a source of therapy for me. In my broken state, I woke up daily with an attitude of Gratitude by giving thanks to my father above for another day of life. I listened to Gospel Songs by Travis Greene, Marvin Sap, Donnie McClurkin, Sinach, and Tasha Cobb, to name a few.

Some people spend countless amounts of money on Counsellors trying to get over the damages incurred by the Narcissist/Karmic Twin as an aftermath of the Final Discard. In my case, my Karmic Twin had become my "fix" for a long time. I made up my mind finally that I will not be waiting in his "Drug Chamber" when he returns to hoover me for supply. I knew I had to kick up the pieces of my life and move on. I binge-eat to medicate the pain I felt deep down inside, and this began to take a toll on my health – through the onset of

Diabetes and weight gain. This was my wake-up call to do better by me, but the soul tie with the Narcissist was so strong, although I was willing, I was too weak emotionally and mentally to make the necessary changes.

One day while I was going through one of my frequent pity parties, I came across a song – I am I Said:-

"L.A.'s fine, the sun shines most the time, and the feeling is laid back (feeling is laid back ooooo) Palm trees grow, and rents are low Don't you know I keep working my way back….. And I am lost, and I can't even say why."

Mikey Spice

That song touches my soul in more ways than I could imagine, and it was also the catalyst for breaking the soul tie I had with My Karmic Twin/Narcissist. The song and melody resonated with me because "I am a Grenadian girl" born and raised on the small Caribbean Island of Grenada. I am currently living in Toronto as a Canadian Citizen, but at times, I feel like I am lost between two shores and frequently hear the calling of my homeland and ancestors.

The void left by the Narcissist was replaced with love and healing for me. Mikey Spice's soulful reggae voice spoke to my soul and ignited a flame that was lying dormant in the darkest places on my heart and soul. The albums by him were on constant repeat play in my home. I believed his soothing voice was responsible for saving me from the dark whole the Narcissist and his demons had left within me. Like a villain, I fought and plodded my way out of the murky trenches the Narcissist and his demons had put me in, and like a Phoenix, I rose from the ashes of the dry bones. Thank you, Mike Spice; you were my "Ray of Sunlight" and hope in the dark, and wounded world I found myself in. You have become my Twin Ray in the spiritual sense of the word.

Notes

Chapter 10: Kundalini Awakening

"You know that you've healed an issue when you can talk about it, and you're not weeping when you can speak to it and identify the lesson. You know that you've healed an issue when, having gone through that, has a benefit that you live today."
Iyanla Vanzant

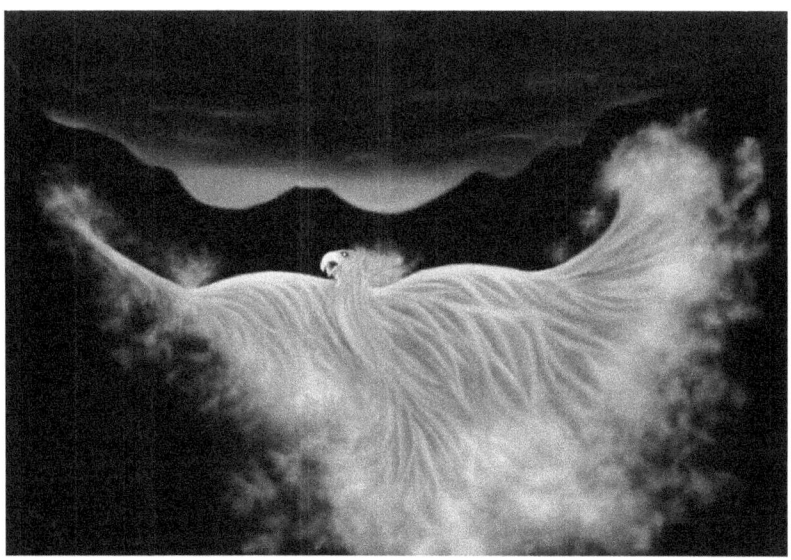

ANSWER THE CALL

I believe the spirit of our ancestors is reenacted in human form in the modern-day, and if a karmic cycle from a past life was not resolved properly, the spirit of the wounded individuals comes back to seek revenge in the present. Have you ever met an individual you never met before or had an interaction with someone and it's like "Dejavu" you swear like you have seen or met the person somewhere before, or you have a strong unexplainable gravitational pull to that person or all the women and men your family dies from the same illness? Do you think it's a coincidence? And what about all the black African Ancestors that tragically died due to slavery – what happened to their spirit and soul? I believe they are still roaming the earth like spirits, and they enter the bodies of people and cause them to act in good or bad ways. In the case of a Soul Mate or Twin Flame from the past who are separated due to tragedy, their souls roam the earth in a human form and somehow due to forces of nature, and the Universe find their way back to each other and tries to complete their love or karmic cycle from the past in present life.

For persons on the Twin Flame or Soulmate journey and are currently separated, the best way to speed up the union process is to be the best version of yourself. Basically, be what you want the King or Queen to be because they intuitively feel everything you are feeling. If you are angry with them or sitting, waiting on them, this will delay the reuniting process. Go out and live your life, meet people and date and do your thing. Fear keeps people stuck in unhealthy relationships, making it harder to move on because one or both parties have codependency and narcissistic tendencies that they have not dealt with. Healing from the past is important in order to enjoy a healthy union.

If union occurs before healing happens and one of the partners is a Narcissist and the other a (codependent and healed) at the end of the day, the one who is healed comes away feeling drained because the unhealed person zaps all their energy and strength out of the other. Instead of both coming to each other with their cups filled, one comes fully because of the healing they have undergone while the other's cup is empty. The one with the empty cup comes into the relationship expecting love and validation from the other without reciprocating the process. Like a bank account, if there are more withdrawals than there are deposits, a deficit or overdraft occurs. The same principle applies to a relationship where one takes more and gives less; after a while, the giver will feel used in the relationship and, due to self-preservation, be forced to withdraw themselves and their love from the relationship, which will then leave the receiver in a state of bewilderment wondering what happened to all the abundance they were receiving. What was happening is that the receiver was like an Energy Vampire sucking the life out of the giver and, therefore, they maintain control in the relationship. The Narcissist will replay the three stages of narcissistic abuse – love bomb, devaluation, and discard to keep their partner hooked in their web of deceit, betrayal, and abuse.

With the Age of the Aquarius, the Universe is trying to reunite Twin Flames, whether by means of a Soul Mate or Life Partner connection. I liken the reunification of the Twin Flame process with that of a butterfly going through the metamorphous process from lava to Caterpillar. Trauma is the energy that fuels the painful birthing processes, and it takes endurance, faith, perseverance, and resilience to be able to make it through the journey.

Trauma from the past, if not healed or dealt with, shows its ugly head in the present and plays out in the Twin Flame, Soul Mate, and Life Partner relationships. Trauma makes people operate from a "Low Vibrational Level," which causes people to behave toxically. Persons operating from a low vibration can intentionally or unintentionally hurt the loved ones in their life as the saying goes, **"hurt people, hurt people,"** but there comes a time when you have to **love yourself more** than you love the toxic person and therefore walk away to do the necessary healing required. You have to go inside and reconnect with a source to operate from a high vibration. In so doing, you learn to forgive and learn to be patient with the growth of another being and yourself.

At times, the ego tries to get in the way of the healing process, and one twin tries to rush the other person's healing process because of how the other person makes them feel. However the Universe sends us back there to learn the lessons over and over again.

Our Twin is meant to teach us life lessons and mirror/trigger the things in us that need change. The toxic energy and resistance of the other person really drain us, but at the end of the day, it all has to do with self-love, temperance, and energizing our chakras. Trauma from our childhood is the main reason for persons vibrating at a low level. The" Inner Child" has been wounded and is in need of self-love. Trauma causes people to be trauma bonded, which later leads to soul ties being formed; these two factors result in cause and effect in relations displayed as Codependency and Narcissism.

To be able to understand the wounding of the soul, it's best to go back to the bible when God made man and breath into him the breath of life. The bible teaches us that human beings have a body, soul, and spirit; the word "soul" is a unification of the body and spirit.

Some believe that when God made man, the soul was split into two and become separated and are therefore roaming until they come together again to mirror each other to bring about the necessary healing to achieve a particular soul purpose that God and the Universe have in store for them. The splitting and unification of souls is what some call Twin Flame Journey

A good way to get over the defeat of the valley experiences that happened in the past is to forget about looking back and go forth towards the higher calling. God builds infrastructure before he brings life – a man who builds a house on an unsteady foundation will fail; the foundation has to be strong enough to hold up the house. In my case, God blew onto the dry bones of my deepest childhood pain and caused a transformation in my life. The spirit of my ancestors rose up in me and revived my wounded spirit, and like a butterfly, I emerged out of my trappings and flapped my wings, and soared high above my trauma after going through the various metamorphosis phases of my life.

<u>FINDING PURPOSE</u>

I trust and believe that as I release my ego and learn to rely on God that one day he will send me my Twin Ray, so in the meantime, I will continue to stay positive by raising my vibrational frequency and insulating my aura from future Narcissists who may try to penetrate it. I am coming to the realization that my Karmic Twin was placed in my life to mirror to me the parts of myself that were in need of change. Now that his purpose in my life has been fulfilled, my healing is preparing me to meet the other half of my soul that God truly meant for me to meet. I think that God, in His infinite wisdom, knew that in my unhealed state, I would have jeopardized the plan and purpose he had for us to be fulfilled as a power couple. I am currently enjoying the series "Dear Wifey" and "Black Love" on YouTube by soaking in love and learning from black couples all over the world.

There were times I was tempted to jump into relationships to fill the void I felt deep down inside, but I knew this would only delay my healing. Therefore I plunged into things that distract me; in the midst of my healing is where I found my purpose - to be a Life Coach and help heal persons out there who are still wounded like I once was.

Mind you, during this time, I was still trauma bonded and soul tied to my Narc, but I busied myself in Reiki, Coaching and counseling workshops, and attended zoom training sessions for my business ventures. Today I am a certified Life Coach, Counsellor, and Reiki Healer and also proud Unfranchised owner of ca.shop.com/Highvibrationlevel and shopglobal.com/Highvibrationlevel. Customers have the opportunity to purchase health, beauty, pet, and household products from my site at reasonable prices while receiving cash back at the same time. I listened to the small voice of God as he sent me life lessons in the form of Narcissism and Codependency to mold me into the vessel that I am today, and for that, I am truly grateful and give Him thanks and praise for his continual blessings in my life.

Sometimes I am tempted to look back at where I have been and how far I came, but I hear the voice of God saying, "continue plodding on, I am proud of the woman you have become, don't be like the woman in the bible who looked back and turned into a pillar of salt. I have work for you to do on this earth, just as you are becoming awakened daily. I want you to help people become awaken too. The next step I have for you is to write a book, and that book will propel you into places to help heal my wounded chosen ones like you, who are also on the journey of enlightenment. Go forth your lessons and tests are completed and become a beacon of light in this dark and wounded world." And to which I responded, "God let not my will be done, but Your will be done in my life, and I am confident that You will give me the tools and put people in my life that will assist me on the path that you have chosen for me."

I must say thus far that God has sent mentors in my life, which is one of the greatest blessings He has bestowed on me. Lately, because the knowledge I have gained is immeasurable. I am truly blessed to have been touched by other angels in human form on my journey to greatness. To the valuable pillars in my life who are too numerous to mention, I want to take this opportunity to say a big '**THANK YOU**". Without you, I don't know where I will be today. You allowed me to be me, and never once did you try to change me into what you thought I should be. You were a shoulder for me to cry on, and no matter how many times I called your phone complaining about the same things when the trials of life knocked me down, you were always there to listen and give me positive advice. Although we both know that I knew what the answer was or what I needed to do, you never rejected or abandoned me, and for that, I am truly grateful. For the angels on YouTube whom I binged watched for hours as they talked on the impact of victims of Narcissism and Codependency or the Twin Flame Journey and to the countless pages of books, I have cried on as I was healing the wounds of Narcissism and letting go of Codependency and enabling tendencies.

Although some of us are brave enough to go through a soul journey, we still live in a 3D world, and it's all about finding a level of balance for life. Staying grounded to Source is all about finding a sense of passion. Passion for some might be gardening for others; it might be traveling to different places. For me, it's listening to music and dancing.

Listening to the gospel and conscious music lifts my soul. However, dancing to Soca music frees me up and causes me to imaginatively float in green pastures where I feel the sun on my face while energetically vibrating to the drums of my ancestors.

When I speak to fellow Caribbean friends of mine who look forward to yearly Carnival experiences in the Caribbean and throughout the world, they tell me they feel the same way. It's like you leave the cares of the world behind that were stressing you for 355 days, and you free up yourself for about 10 days where at the end, you come away on a euphoric high, invigorated and ready to face the world. For me, the pulsating sounds and rhythm of the "Jab Jab" music resonate deep with my bones that it makes me swirl and twirl to the intoxicating aroma of the musical hertz.

I look forward to yearly carnival experiences like Caribana, and Greenz Carnival to name a few to have musical juices flowing. Ubersoca Cruise is a cruise where most of the Soca Artist from all over the Caribbean come together, and Caribbean people and friends alike gravitate in one space for 5 days and connect and "whine" to the pulsating sounds of "SOCA." The joys you feel during those

experiences are a wonder to behold and can only be truly experienced if you let go of your judgments and inhibitions and let the sound of the music enter through the ears and the eyes and then flows through all the Chakras of the body. At this point, you are oblivious to the inquisitive stares of onlookers because I am at one with the Soca and Jab Jab music which to me feels like my ancestors speaking to me through music. I felt this same eutrophic feeling when I decided to throw caution and fears to the winds and reach out in faith to start an online shop and coaching business.

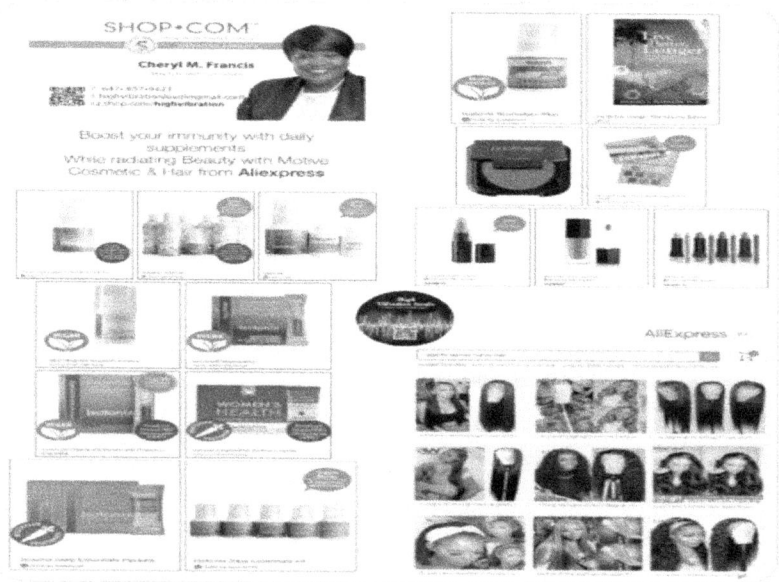

In the words of one of my favorite soca artist:-

"**Boss Lady**", I come for this work, sign me up..........
You say you have a vacancy
I go be Number one employee
I am to please Guaranteed
I fit and ready
Ah right here
Well-equipped
You structure
I climbing it
This economy has looking for wuk, **boss lady**."
Kes The Band

www.highvibrationlevel.com

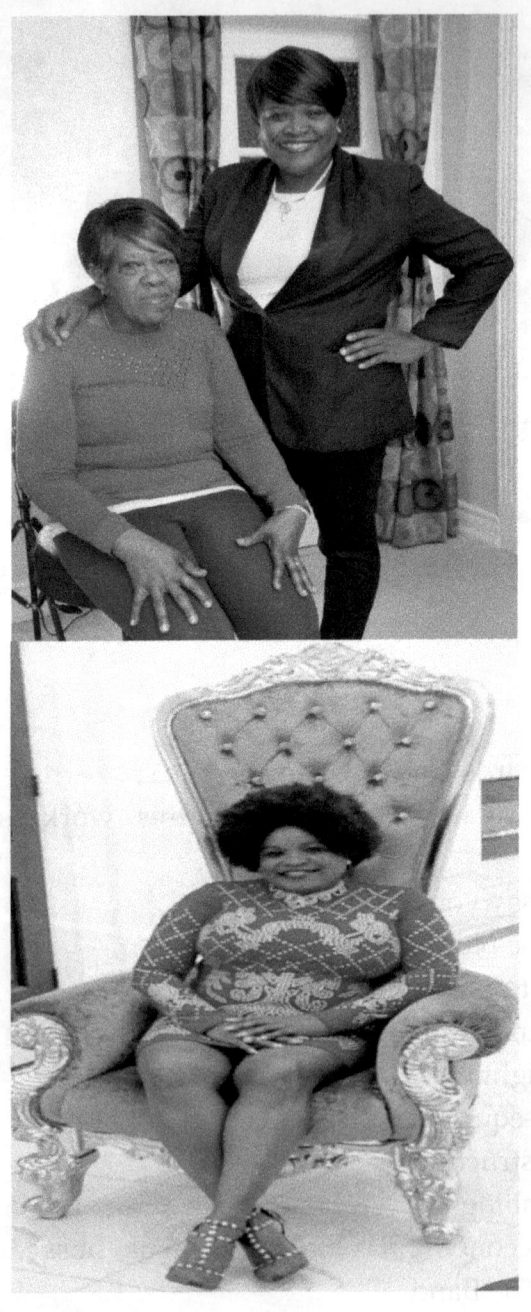

www.highvibrationlevel.com

Life is a journey, and we should not be afraid to take the plunge and enjoy the twist and turns that lie ahead. With God's grace and the protection of our ancestors, we will be OK.

THE END

Notes

www.highvibrationlevel.com

The journey is finally over, and I know it was a lot of "food for thought" don't worry below is a summary of the key ideas from each chapter which is covered in the book; you can return to it at any time.

In this book, you would be able to reflect upon the following:

Chapter 1 Parent Child Relationship
- Childhood Wounding
- Attachment Styles
- Role Reversal
- Child Abuse
- Abandonment
- Detachment

Chapter 2 Codependency and Narcissism
- Trauma Bonding
- People Pleasing
- Low Self Esteem
- Lack of Boundaries
- Mental Health Disorder
- Cognitive Dissonance

Chapter 3 Trauma
- Alcoholism
- Sexual Abuse
- Drug Abuse
- Physical Abuse
- Religion
- Tradition

Chapter 4 Dark Night of the Soul
- Unrequited Love
- Denial
- Pain
- Death of the Ego
- Isolation

- Forgiveness

Chapter 5 Self Love
- Acceptance
- No Contact
- Healthy Boundaries
- Listening to the Inner Voice
- Connecting to Source
- Self-care

Chapter 6 Healing
- Pray
- Deliverance
- Mindful Meditation
- Chakra Healing
- Inner Child Healing
- Therapy

Chapter 7 Ying and Yang
- Mirroring
- Divine Masculine and Divine Feminine
- Twin Flame
- Soul Shock
- Shapeshifting
- Balance

Chapter 8 Let Go and Let God
- Surrender
- Be Gentle with Yourself
- Acceptance of a Greater Power
- Diving Timing
- PUSH
- Learn the Lesson

Chapter 9 Breakthrough

- o Rise from the Ashes
- o Intuition
- o Clairvoyance
- o Awakened
- o Third Eye
- o Lesson learned

Chapter 10 Kundalini Awakening
- o Answer The Call
- o Connected to Ancestors
- o Identify Life Purpose
- o Go After the Purpose
- o Connect with Soul Tribe
- o Enlighten Others

www.highvibrationlevel.com

About the Author

Cheryl M. Francis was born in the "Isles of Spice," a tiny island in the Caribbean called Grenada but currently resides in Toronto, Canada; has a Master's Degree in Business Administrations and International Business from St. George's University, a first degree in Management Studies from the University of the West Indies and a Diploma in International Transportation and Logistics from Seneca College. She has also decided to upgrade her skill set with courses in Coaching and Reiki from recognized organizations and recently became a franchise owner of an online business.

The author is available for Coaching, Reiki, sales, and keynote presentations to appropriate audiences. For bookings and rates, please contact the author directly at: highvibrationlevel@gmail.com or via websites:-

      highvibrationlevel.com
      shopGlobal.com/highvibration
      ca.shop.com/highvibration

Book can be purchased by doing a search for "A Heroine's Journey" on Amazon.com and other internet platforms.

Finally, if the writings in this book have connected with you on a soul level, please honor others with your knowledge by purchasing an extra copy, and pass it on to your friends and family as a gift so their soul too might be uplifted and enlightened.

www.highvibrationlevel.com

www.ingramcontent.com/pod-product-compliance
Lightning Source LLC
Chambersburg PA
CBHW071221160426
43196CB00012B/2364